DATE DUE

AN EARLY CRAFT BOOK

DOLL HOUSES

by KARIN KELLY *pictures by* GEORGE OVERLIE

745.5
KEL

GARDEN HOMES
6745
SCHOOL LIBRARY

Lerner Publications Company • Minneapolis, Minnesota

LIBRARY OF CONGRESS CATALOGING IN PUBLICATION DATA

Kelly, Karin.
Doll houses.

(An Early Craft Book)
SUMMARY: Instructions for making a doll house from a cardboard box and furnishing it with objects made from spools, fabric, clay, cardboard, and other materials. Also includes dollmaking and other projects.

1. Doll houses—Juvenile literature. 2. Doll furniture—Juvenile literature. 3. Dollmaking—Juvenile literature. [1. Doll houses. 2. Dollmaking. 3. Handicraft] I. Overlie, George, illus. II. Title.

TT175.3.K44 745.59'23 72-13338
ISBN 0-8225-0854-0

Copyright © 1974 by Lerner Publications Company

ISBN No. 0-8225-0854-0
Library of Congress No. 72-13338
Printed in U.S.A.

Contents

A doll house is you 5

The floor plan 9

Tools and materials 10

Building the house 12

Fill the empty rooms 19

Tools and materials 19

Furniture and decor 22

Who lives here? 30

Other projects 31

A doll house made in 1774

A doll house is you

When we are young, many of the games we play are imitations of the things grown-ups do. We pretend that we are secret agents, or airplane pilots, or explorers under the sea. The grown-ups we imitate may change with the times. Different kinds of heroes and heroines appeal to each generation. For example, Tom Sawyer liked pirates. Boys and girls today might like to pretend that they are traveling through space to the moon and stars.

But there is one game that has changed very little in thousands of years. That game is playing house. Every one of us seems to want to make a home life that we can control and organize ourselves. And a doll house is a perfect and beautiful home. We can build it, put furniture in it, and run it as we like. By making a doll house, we can also prepare for the home life we will have some day when we are grown.

In the past, parents often made or bought doll houses for their children so that they *could* learn how to make and keep a home. This was a good idea because we learn as much at play as we do at work.

Today, however, people want to learn more than the way things were done in the past. We want to learn how to keep the earth and its people safe and healthy. We want to learn how to make the world a better place in which to live. Learning new things means that we experiment with new ideas more freely.

So, when we build and play with our doll houses, we can feel free to do anything we want with them. We can keep them clean and ordered in any way we want. We can make them any kind of house, and they can look like anything we choose. And this is a good idea too. We can build houses with flower-printed roofs, doll houses that look like cozy tree-trunk houses, or tiny "mouse houses." We can build houses to fit any mood or personality.

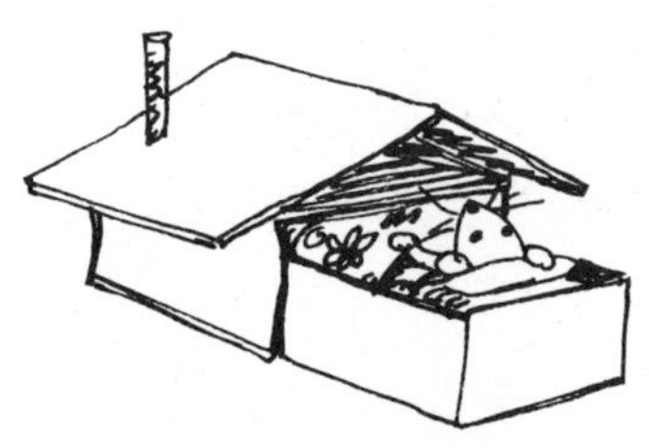

I do not want to teach you the "right way" to make a doll house. I only want to show you how to make houses and furniture that are sturdy and strong. When you have a sturdy house and tables and chairs that can be moved around many times, I'm sure that you will invent a "life style" that suits you.

Just as your doll house will show the kind of life style you like, the doll houses of the past show how those people lived. Many of the doll houses in museums are very rich and formal. These doll houses were often made for the children of wealthy people, and they were often the work of skilled craftsmen.

One such doll house, the famous Queen's Doll House, can be seen in a royal palace, Windsor Castle, in England. This doll house is perfect in every detail. It has running water and a wine cellar with real wine. The beds, pictures, and books are so real looking that photographs of them fool the eye.

Our doll houses, or at least my doll houses, are not as elaborate and perfect. I am not an elaborate person, and I am not a perfect housekeeper. My mother is a perfect housekeeper. If she built a doll house, it would be neater than mine. Are you neater than I? Are you more casual than I? You will learn something about yourself when you make a doll house.

Let's begin with a simple doll house, one that you can change to fit your tastes. If you like, your doll house can be an apartment in a large building. It can be a house in a small town, or a farm home. It will have bedrooms, a bathroom, a kitchen, a place to eat, and a place to relax.

If we are to have all these rooms, we should take care to follow one "rule." We should build our house "to scale." This means that we should build rooms and furniture that are properly proportioned. We would not want a giant chair in a tiny living room or a tiny stove in a giant kitchen.

You will find that, as you build, you will enter the new, smaller world you are creating. If you are careful with the sizes of furniture and rooms, your world will be more pleasing to look at and to "live in." You will not have to "climb up" to your chair or "bend over" a very low stove. The easiest scale to work with is one in which one inch of doll house space equals one foot of normal space.

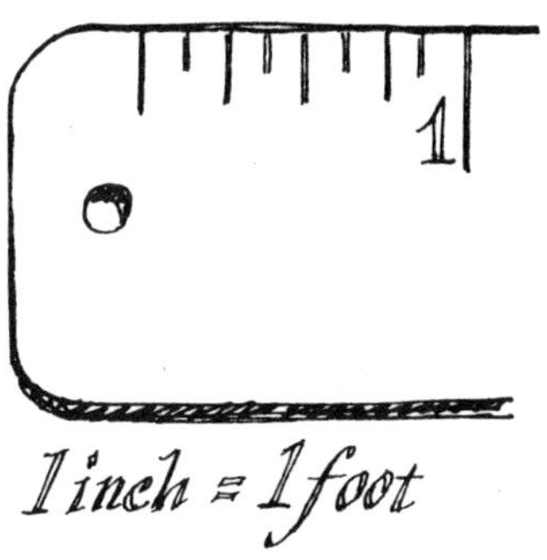

The floor plan

Shall we put our building together? Let's start with a two-story house. Later, if you like, you can join larger units together to make houses that have several stories and "wings." The two bedrooms and bath will be "upstairs," and the living room, dining room, and kitchen "downstairs." If you have room, you can add a hall on the bottom floor with stairs that lead up to a hall on the top floor. Your plans, however, will depend upon the space you have to work with. If you don't have much space, it is often easier to pretend that there are doors, halls, and stairways.

Tools and materials

These are the tools and materials you will need to assemble the building:

large cardboard box

a large sturdy cardboard box. (It should be at least 13 to 15 inches deep, 16 to 20 inches long, and 12 to 16 inches across to provide enough space for six rooms.)

a package of brass paper fasteners (brads)

several large pieces of corrugated cardboard (about two feet by two feet

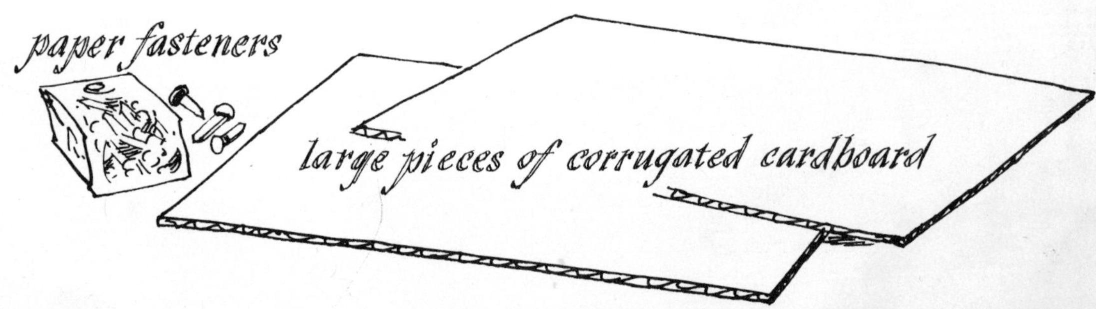

—larger still if you want to use a piece of cardboard for a yard around your house)

a large sheet of poster board

white contact paper

masking tape

white glue

a pencil

a one-foot ruler

an X-acto knife (You can buy one at a hobby shop.)

a large pair of scissors

colored construction paper or printed wrapping paper

green and/or brown burlap (if you want a yard and/or a patio)

white flat-wall paint and a brush.

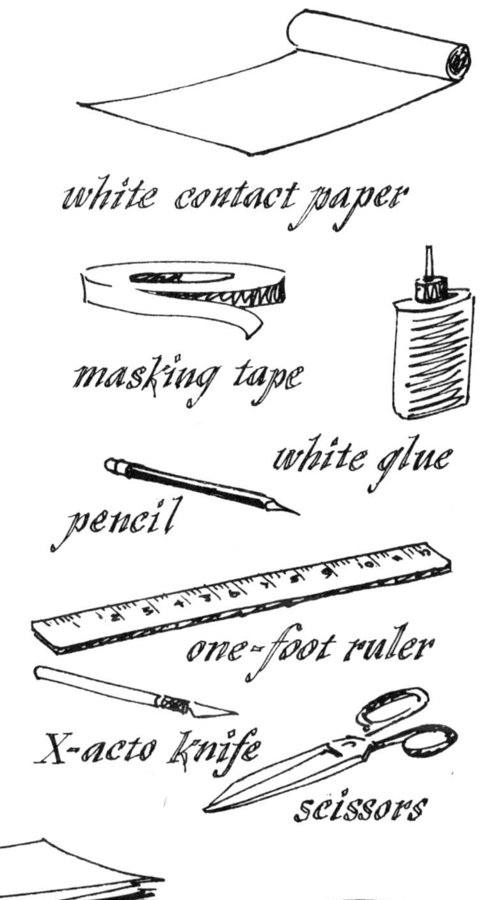

Building the house

To begin, cut the end flaps away from the cardboard box and turn the box so that it sits on one of its long sides. Then, after you have measured the distance of the long side, cut out a piece of corrugated cardboard that is one inch longer than the long side and one inch shorter than the depth of the box. You will use this piece of cardboard to make a floor divider. Draw a line one-half inch in from each end of the cardboard slab and fold the cardboard along these lines.

Now measure the height of the ends of the box and divide that measurement exactly in half. This will give you the division between the top and bottom stories of your house. Draw a line on the outside of the box to mark this division and make three pencilled "Xs" at equally spaced points along the line. Make "Xs" at exactly the same places on the fold of the cardboard floor divider. Puncture each "X" (on

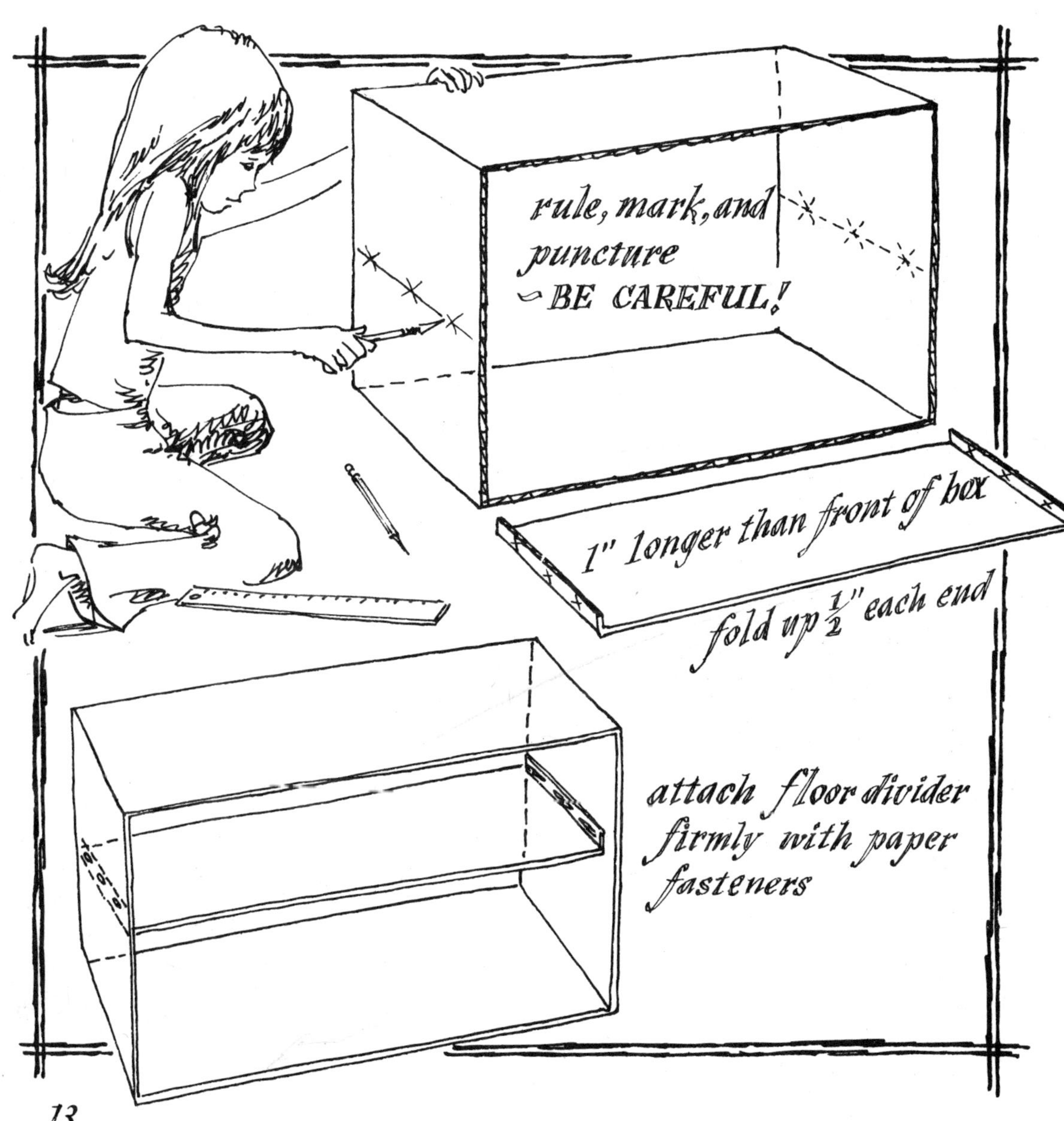
rule, mark, and
puncture
~BE CAREFUL!
1" longer than front of box
fold up ½" each end
attach floor divider
firmly with paper
fasteners

both box and cardboard) with the X-acto knife. Please work carefully with that knife, and please keep your fingers away from the blade. It is very sharp, so you should ask a grown-up for help.

When you have made holes in both ends of the box and the floor divider, you can fasten the floor divider inside of the box. Use the paper fasteners. Push them through the holes from the outside to the inside and spread the legs of the fasteners so that the floor is firm and sturdy.

cover inside of box with white contact paper

Now you can prepare the house for windows and rooms. Begin by papering the closed end of the box on the inside with white contact paper. This will cover the folds in the cardboard so that the back walls of the house will be smooth. Apply the contact paper as carefully as you can so that it does not wrinkle or form air bubbles. When you have papered, you may begin to cut the windows.

Measure the windows on the outside of the box. The pencil line you made for the floor divider will guide you when you decide where the windows should go. Make a house with lots of windows. Make at least three windows for each large room and one small window for the bath. When you have measured and drawn guidelines for all of the windows, cut them out with the X-acto knife. Again, please be careful. Better yet, get help.

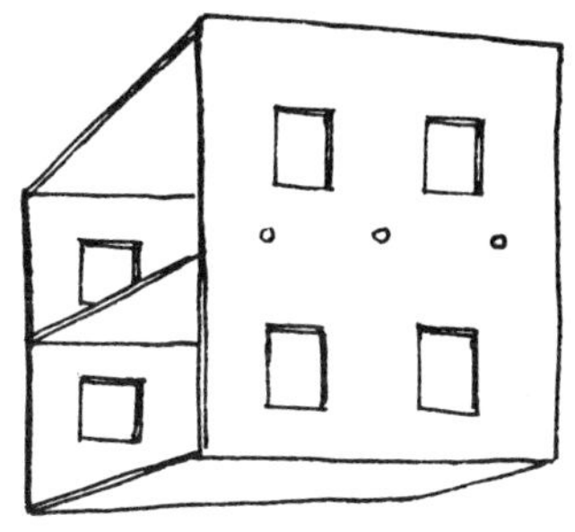

window openings at sides of house

When the windows are cut, use strips of contact paper like tape and cover the rough edges of the box around the windows and at the open end of the house. You can make window panes out of cellophane wrap at a later stage in construction.

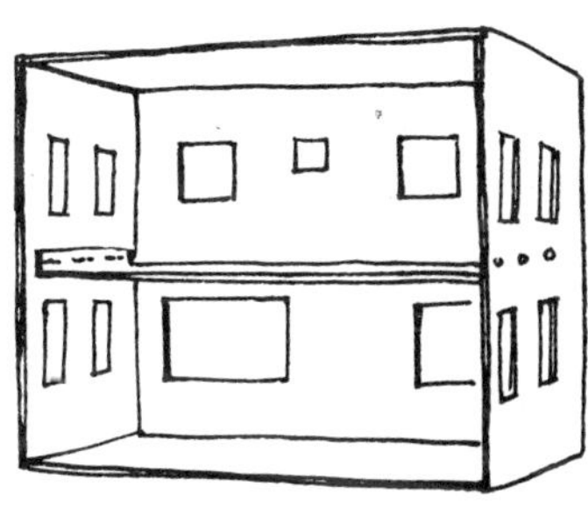

window openings at rear of house

After you finish the windows, you may put in the room dividers. On the top floor, you can do away with the need for doors to each room by leaving a three-inch hall at the open end of the house. Therefore, the room dividers will be three inches shorter than the floor divider.

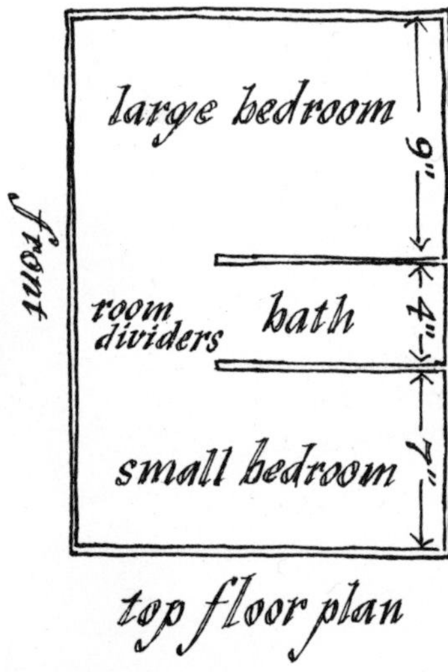

top floor plan

bottom floor plan

Putting in the room dividers will give you a chance to be an architect. For example, on the top floor, you might want three rooms—a large bedroom, a smaller bedroom and a bathroom. You might like to put the bathroom in between the two bedrooms. Your dolls could get to it by way of the hall at the open end of the house. If your house is 20 inches across, your large bedroom can be nine inches wide, your bath four inches wide, and your small bedroom seven inches wide. Use the ruler and pencil to mark off these room divisions.

On the bottom floor, try using an L-shaped area that will be a combination of living room and dining room. You will need only one wall to separate this area from the kitchen. If the house is 20 inches across, the kitchen could be seven inches wide and the living and dining area 13 inches wide. Measure and mark the bottom floor for the wall separating these rooms.

Then measure and cut the room dividers out of cardboard. Remember that they should be

GARDEN HOMES SCHOOL LIBRARY

three inches shorter than the floor dividers. They should also be as tall as the ceilings and should fit snugly, so don't cut them too small.

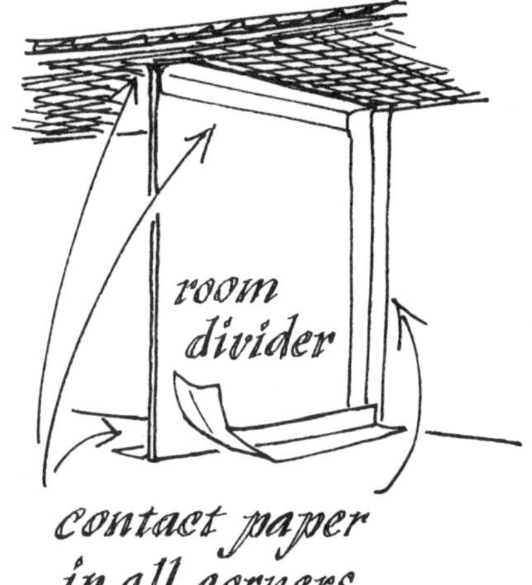

Attach the room dividers with masking tape or with strips of contact paper. Contact paper is better if you can manage it, because you can paint over it easily. 745.5 - KEL

Now the house is ready for a roof. This is how you might add a peaked roof. Cut out two lengths of corrugated cardboard as long as the house is. The pieces should be wide enough to make a gentle slope when they are joined together at the top. Tape the pieces together and fold them at the tape line. Then tape the roof firmly to the edges of the top of the house.

There will be an empty triangle at each end of the roof. Cut poster-board triangles to fill these spaces and tape them in firmly with strips of contact paper or masking tape. 6745

Now you've done it! The basic structure of your first doll house is complete. Give the whole thing two coats of white paint and let it dry thoroughly before you continue.

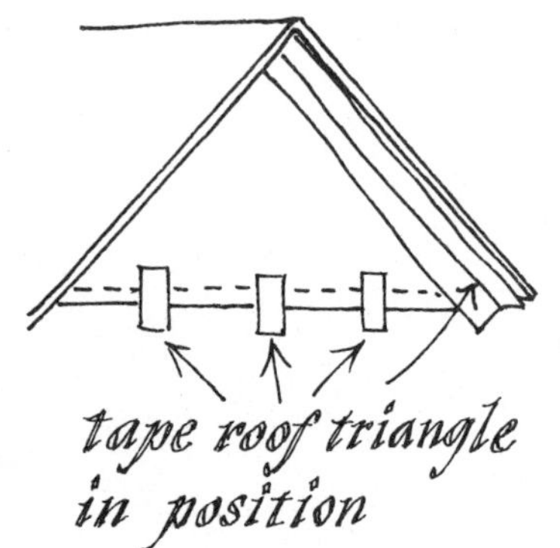

Is it cool and quiet on the inside of the doll house? Are you pleased with it? Look at it for a while and think about the many possibilities for finishing it.

You might want to put roofing and shutters on the house at this point. You can cover the roof with sheets of colored or printed paper. Or you can cut "shingles" from the paper and attach them one by one, with each shingle slightly overlapping its neighbor. You can make shutters from colored paper or painted corrugated cardboard.

To make a yard for your house, cover one side of a large square of corrugated cardboard (at least six inches larger than the size of the bottom floor of the house) with green burlap. Glue the burlap down with white glue. If you want to use part of the yard as a patio, cover that part with brown burlap. You might want to leave the yard as a separate piece instead of attaching it to the house. This would make the doll house easier to store.

Fill the empty rooms

bedside table with perfume bottle lamp

Now it is time to think about decorating the walls and making furniture. The possibilities for furniture and interior decor are too numerous, perhaps, to be contained in any book. Your doll house furniture can look like real furniture, or it can be a simple shape that suggests a function. A single cup from an egg carton, for example, could be painted or covered with cloth and turned upside down to suggest a stool or a bedside table. You could mold clay into the inside of another cup and use it for a bathroom sink. In furnishing our doll house, we will work with both kinds of furniture—real-looking furniture and creative odds and ends.

bathroom sink

Tools and materials

These are the tools and materials you will need to make some basic pieces of furniture and accessories for your doll house:

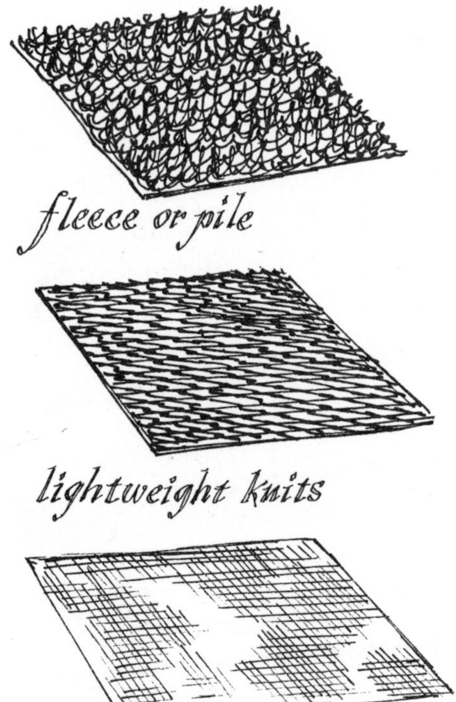

scraps of cloth. Your mother or a friend might have scraps of cloth you can use. It is also great fun to go to a fabric shop and buy the colors and textures you like. All you will need are pieces of fabric one-eighth of a yard long, so you can furnish your entire house for a few dollars. You might like:

fleece or acrylic pile for carpets

lightweight knits for upholstery and pillows

lightweight cotton for curtains

wool and terrycloth for scatter rugs

printed contact paper for wall paper

a large sheet of poster board

double-coated tape (tape that is sticky on both sides)

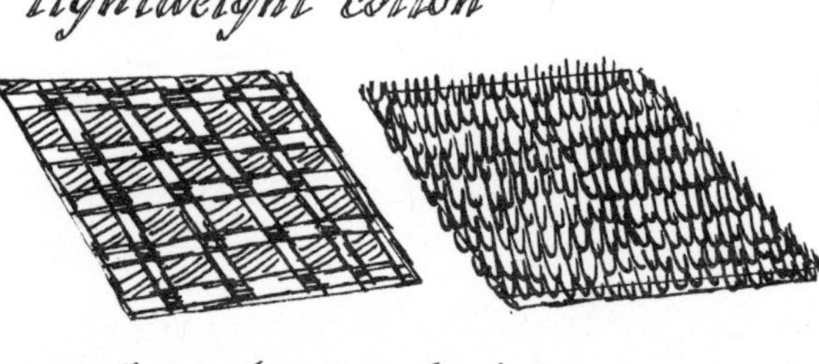

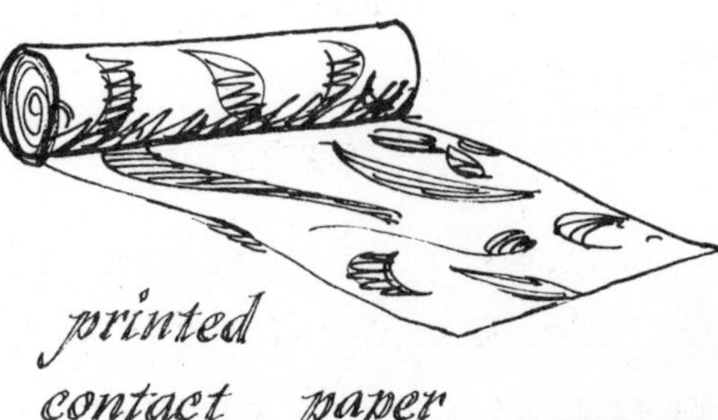

white glue

a roll of cotton

tempera paints, especially brown for "wooden" furniture

acrylic modeling clay

beads

fringes and bits of lace for curtains

thumb tacks

needles and thread

a pencil

a ruler

scissors

an X-acto knife

pipe cleaners

colored construction paper

a black felt-tipped pen.

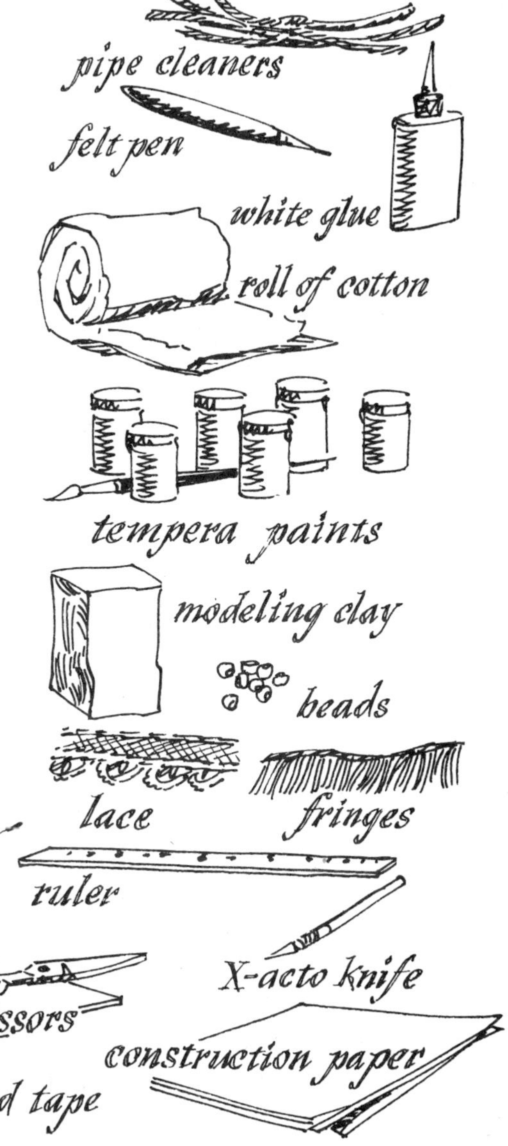

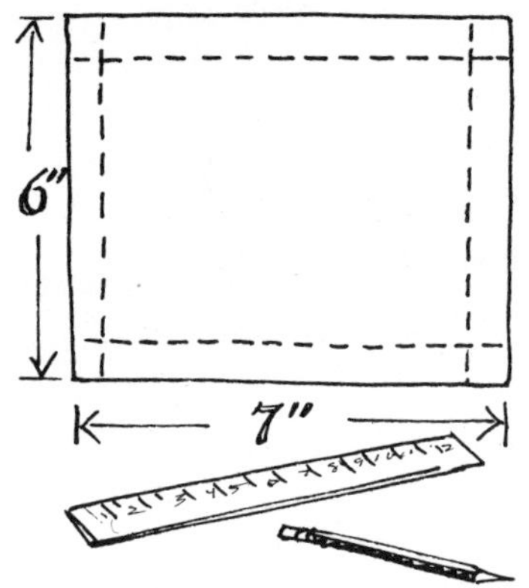

Furniture and decor

Before you actually install furniture in your doll house, you should paint or put wall paper where you wish. You should also carpet the floors. Carpeting made from heavy fabrics looks nice. Choose the colors that you like and cut the fabrics to fit each room. You can cut an L-shaped piece to cover your entire dining room/ living room space. When the carpet is cut to size, glue it down with white glue. When you have finished this basic work, the rooms will be ready for furniture.

Let's make a large, soft bed first. We will begin with a basic box shape. You can use this box as the beginning for many, many different pieces of doll-house furniture.

To make a bed that is five inches long, four inches wide, and one inch high, measure and cut out a piece of poster board that is seven inches long and six inches wide. Measure and draw lines one inch in from each edge of this piece. Then, on the short ends of the rectangle, cut on the one-inch lines from the edge of the piece to the point where the lines cross.

Fold the rectangle on all of the lines. Fold the small end flaps over the large end flaps and tape them together firmly with double-coated tape. Put the tape between the flaps so that it does not show. You will see that you have made a flat box.

To make this box into a bed, you should first add some cotton padding for a mattress. Cut out a piece of cotton that is as large as the top of the box and glue it on with white glue. Then cut out a piece of fabric that is eight inches long and seven inches wide. Cut a two-inch slash at each corner in this piece of cloth. Place it over the top of the bed and fold each corner neatly around the corners of the bed. Tuck the ends in to make neat folds, and glue the extra cloth to the underside of the bed.

Now you can make some pillows. Cut two rectangles, four and one-half inches by two and three-fourths inches, from a fabric that matches

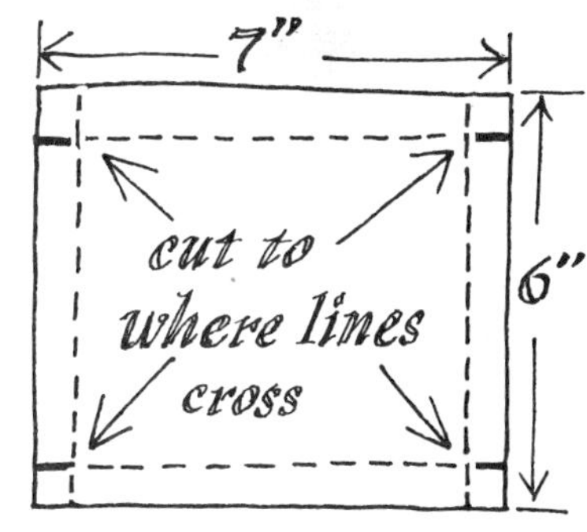

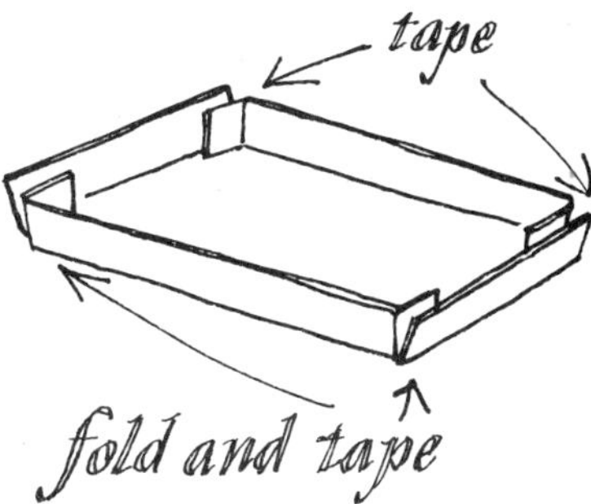

cloth 8"x 7"

stuff with cotton

fold under and
glue to underside

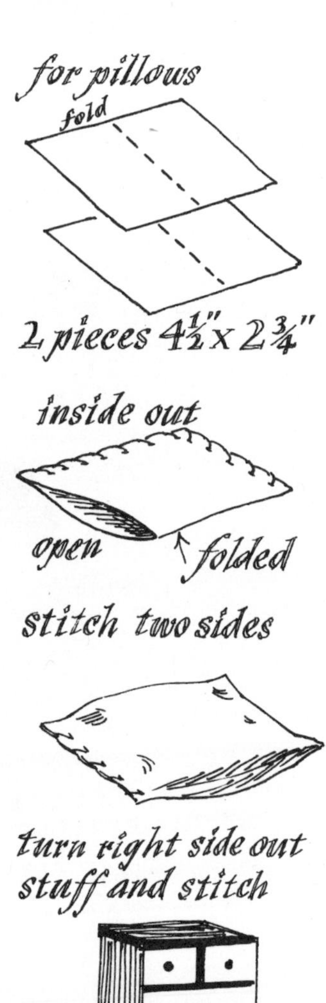

the bedspread. Fold the pieces in half, wrong side out. Then stitch two of the three open sides of the pillows together (one side will be a fold), and turn the pillows right side out. Stuff them with cotton and stitch the open sides.

The bed is finished! Does it look comfy? Put it in the largest bedroom. Make a narrower bed, like a single bed, for the smaller bedroom.

Make chests of drawers with the basic box, paint them with tempera paint, and draw in drawer lines with the felt-tipped pen. Put an aluminum foil mirror above a low chest of drawers, and frame it with painted poster board. Make a clothes trunk or toy chest to put at the foot of the narrow bed.

You can make another narrow bed and use it as a studio couch in the living room. Or, if you'd like to try something more complicated, you could make an upholstered sofa. Let's try. Let's make a sofa that is five inches long. Begin with a poster-board box that is five inches long, one and one-half inches wide, and one inch high. Upholster this box and cover it with fabric as you did the beds. Then you may add a back and arms.

Cut out a piece of poster board that is five inches long and two inches wide. This will be the back of your sofa. With scissors, round off the top corners. Cut out a strip of cotton and glue it to the top half of the strip of poster board. Cut out a strip of fabric and glue it to the poster board over the cotton and around the top, bottom, and sides of the strip.

When the back is covered with fabric, cut out two one and one-half inch square pieces of poster board for arms. Upholster and cover them as you did the back of the sofa.

Now you can assemble all of the parts of the sofa. Tape the arms and back together around the sides and back of the seat. Use small pieces of tape to fasten the back and arms to the seat on the bottom edge. Then cover the front, sides, and back with a strip of the sofa fabric, cut long enough and wide enough to extend all around the sofa. Cut it in a shape that will fit the height

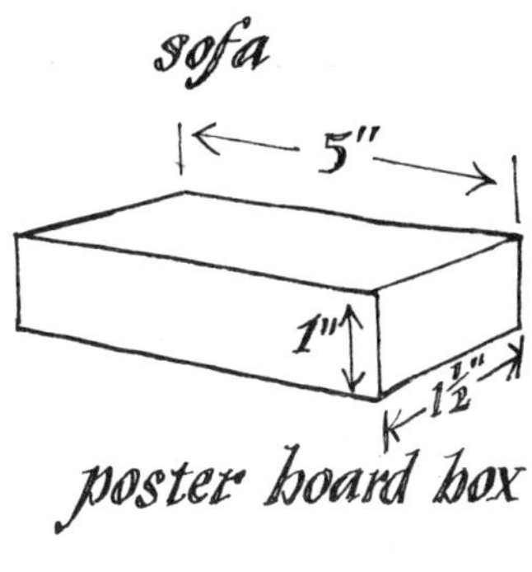

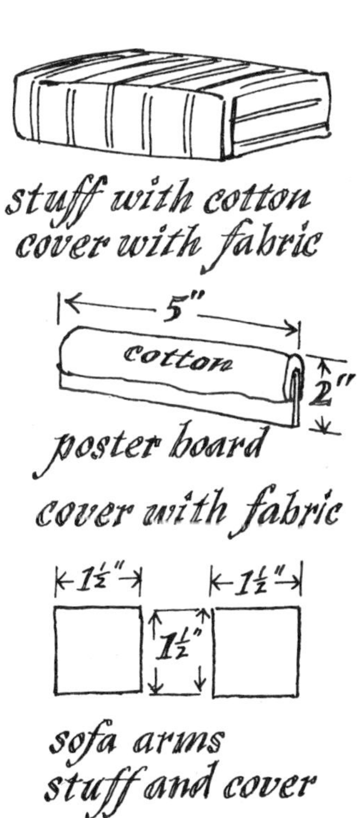

of the back, arms, and front. Glue the fabric strip on with white glue.

tape at bottom

To give your sofa some extra charm, you might like to add a "dust ruffle" around the bottom. One very easy way is to glue on a strip of ball fringe around the sides and front of the sofa. You could also sew a ruffle for the sofa. Cut out a strip of fabric that is one inch wide and 12 inches long. Use a simple in-and-out stitch at the top edge of the strip. When you have stitched the full length of the strip, pull the sewing thread and "gather," or ruffle, the strip until it is as long as the distance around the front and sides of the sofa. Attach the ruffle with tiny stitches or double-coated tape. Make some little pillows for your sofa too.

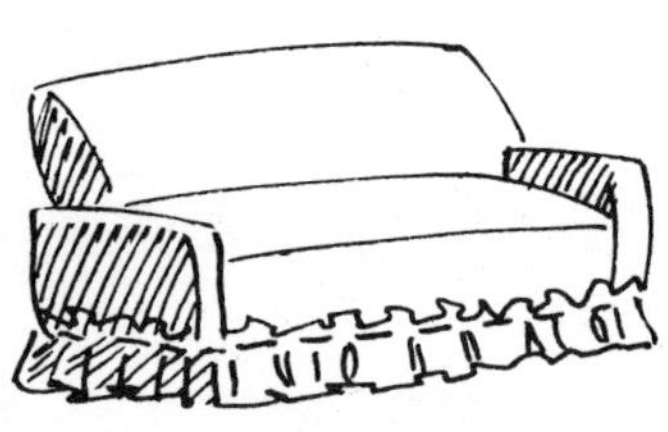

dust ruffle stitched on

You can make upholstered chairs in the same way that you made the sofa. Would you like to make a rocking chair as well? Some people say that real rocking chairs were first made as copies of a doll-house rocking chair.

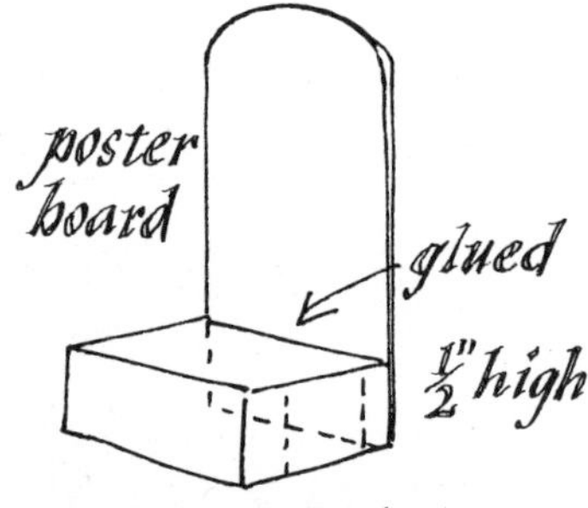

rocking chair

To make a rocking chair, make a box chair with a seat one-half inch tall and with a high back. Now you have to make rockers for your chair. Cut out two strips of poster board that are two inches long and one-half inch wide. Make rounded corners on the edges so that the chair will rock. Cut slits in the top sides of the rockers so that you can insert the rocker seat into them. Paint the chair and the rockers with tempera paint to look like wood. Why don't you make a tiny cushion for the rocking chair seat.

Would you like to put a fireplace in the doll house? Make a basic box out of sandpaper and cut a square hole out of the front and bottom of the box. Use double-coated tape to attach a mantel made of a painted strip of poster board. You can use matchsticks or cut-up soda straws for logs.

Be as creative as you can with odds and ends. A paper cup makes a fine dining room table. Cut the top of the cup away until the cup is about two inches high. Turn it upside down. Then make a pretty table cloth. Use a compass, and measure and cut out a circle of cloth that will cover the table and touch the floor all

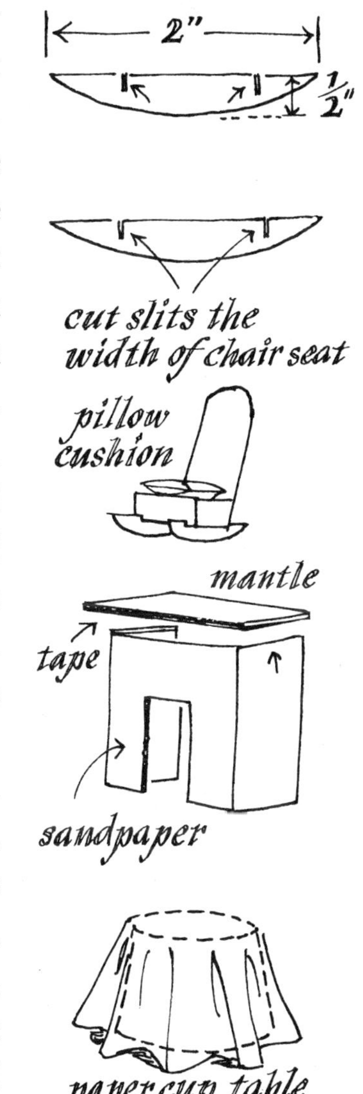

around. Use double-coated tape or white glue and fasten the cloth to the table. Make some "wooden" dining room chairs from poster-board boxes.

Spools can be used for many kinds of stools and tables. To make a footstool, for example, glue a round piece of cotton to the top of a spool. Then measure and cut out a circle of cloth that will be long enough and wide enough to cover the spool and touch the floor. Tie the fabric cover on with a bit of narrow ribbon. To make a table from a spool, simply glue a piece of poster board (round, square, or rectangular) to the top of it.

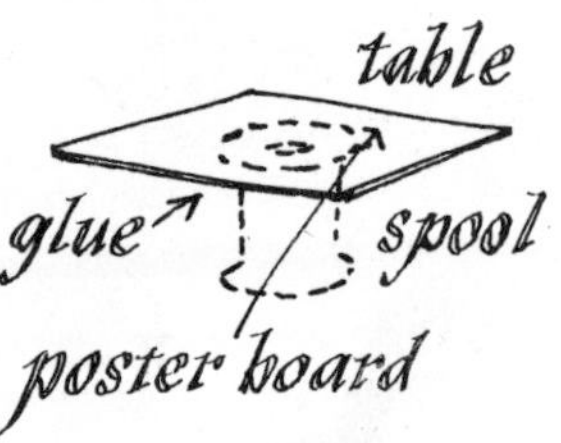

The bathroom is a good place to furnish with odds and ends. A small gift box, painted white or some bright color, would make a fine bath-tub. You could use a spool for a toilet. Perhaps the easiest way to furnish a bathroom is to model the sink, tub, and toilet out of acrylic modeling clay. Before the clay hardens, stick in tiny strips of aluminum foil for faucets and handles. Paint the clay articles when they have

dried. Use a paper clip as a towel rack. Slip tiny pieces of fabric over the prongs on one side and tape the clip to the wall.

To make kitchen appliances (sink, stove, and refrigerator), use gift boxes or poster-board boxes. Draw in lines for doors, drawers, and ovens with a felt-tipped pen. Paste little circles of black paper on top of your stove to look like burners. If you like, you can cover these appliances with printed contact paper.

After you have made all of the furniture and appliances that you need, you may begin to add the finishing touches that will make your house a home. You will probably want curtains for your windows. You can use ball fringe, wide lace, or braid for some windows.

You can also sew ruffled curtains in the same way that you sewed dust ruffles for your upholstered furniture. Attach any of the curtains you choose with thumb tacks. If you feel especially ambitious, you can make curtain rods from toothpicks or matchsticks and sew the curtains to them. Make decorative shades for

kitchen stove

black paper circles

lace curtains

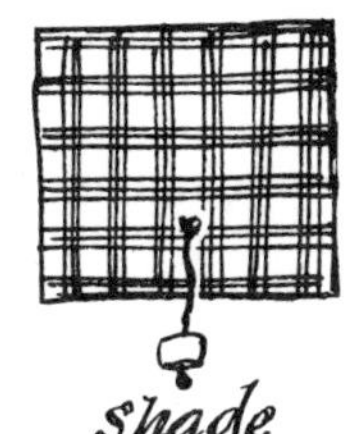

shade

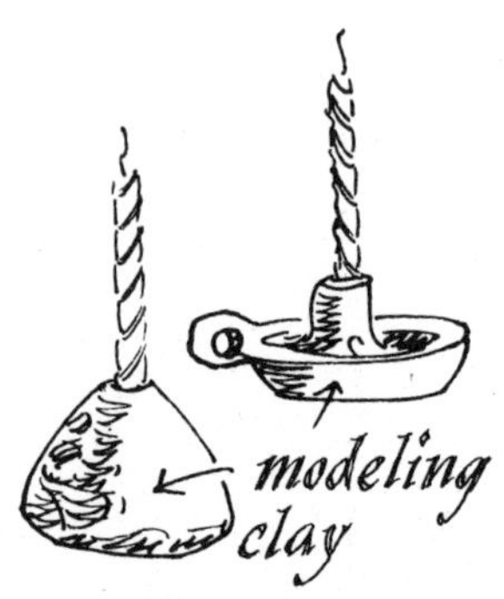

kitchen and bathroom from square pieces of cloth. Sew beads on the shades for shade pulls and attach the tops of the shades to the tops of the windows with glue.

You will need lighting for your rooms too. You can make tiny candle holders from modeling clay. Put birthday candles that have been cut in half in the candle holders.

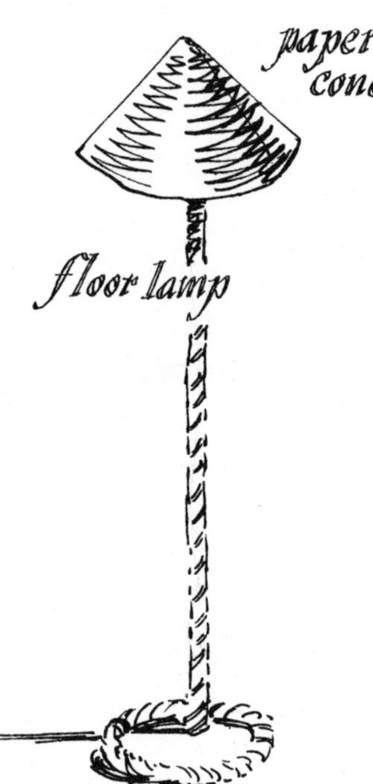

To make a lamp, bend a pipe cleaner in a coil at one end so that it stands by itself. Then cut out a round piece of colored paper for the shade. Glue it together into a cone shape, put a dot of glue at the center of the cone, and attach the shade to the lamp base. Pretty table lamps can be made from tiny perfume bottles and paper cone shades.

Who lives here?

When you have added these last details, your little house will be quite ready for its inhabitants. You can buy dolls at a toy store, or you can make some for yourself. I think spool people are interesting, and they will fit very nicely in the house. To make a spool doll, begin by gluing two leg spools to a body spool.

To make the arms, thread two small spools on a four-and-one-half-inch piece of heavy twine. Cut four mitten-shaped hands out of paper and glue two of them over each loose string at the ends of the spools. Then glue the middle length of string to the top of the body and fasten it even more securely by gluing a head spool on top of it. Paint a face on the head and clothes on the body.

Other projects

Do you have other toy friends who deserve a house of their own? Do you have a tiny toy mouse, or a small bear like Pooh, or some kittens? I have a "family" of tiny ceramic Siamese cats who live in a shoe-box house. It is very small, but it suits them very well. There is a floor divider but no room dividers in the shoe-box house. I painted in rooms with differ-

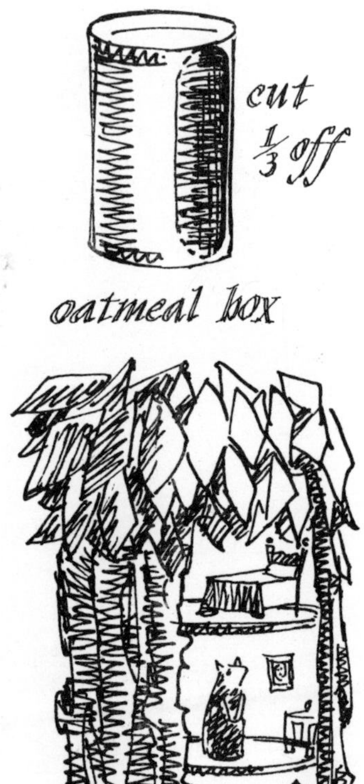

ent colors of paint and made tiny furniture for each room.

Perhaps you'd like a tree-trunk house for some forest friend. Make one out of an oatmeal box. Stand the box upright and cut one-third of it off on one side. Put strips of papier-mâché (paper dipped in paste) all over the outside of the box and paint it brown to look like rough bark and wood. Then put floors in the house, paint it, and furnish it. The tree-trunk house would be a fine "cubbyhole" for Pooh Bear.

There are many things you can do with doll houses and many ways to play with them. They will always awaken and tantalize your imagination. Do you think you could build a Japanese doll house or an Indian teepee? There are many kinds of doll houses that you can build.

And, even when a house seems finished, you may discover that it is never really finished, for you may want to change the decor and make new furnishings again and again. Creating doll houses is a craft you will enjoy long after you have given up your other toys.